CALIFORNIA

Science

Interactive Text

Mc Graw Hill **Macmillan McGraw-Hill**

B

The *McGraw-Hill* Companies

 Macmillan/McGraw-Hill

Send all inquiries to:
Macmillan/McGraw-Hill
8787 Orion Place
Columbus, OH 43240-4027

ISBN: 978-0-02-285999-2
MHID: 0-02-285999-3

Printed in the United States of America.

18 HES 15 14 13 12

Contents

Contents

CHAPTER 1

Plant Life Cycles

The Big Idea How do plants grow and change?

Vocabulary

flowers the parts of plants that make seeds

pollen a sticky powder inside flowers

fruit the part of a plant that keeps seeds safe and helps them grow

seeds the parts of plants that can grow into new plants

life cycle steps that show how a living thing grows, changes, and makes new living things

What do roots, stems, and leaves do?

Plants use their roots, stems, and leaves to get light and water.

Globe Thistle

The stem holds up the plant.

Leaves use light to make food.

Roots hold the plant in the ground. They take in water from the soil.

Read a Diagram

Plants that grow in the rain forest have large leaves. Large leaves help plants take in sunlight.

Desert plants have few leaves. Some desert plants have no leaves. They store water in their thick stems.

banana tree

Joshua tree

✔ Quick Check

1. What do the roots of a plant do?

_____

2. Name a desert plant. _____

How can we describe roots?

Some roots are long and thin. Others are short and thick. Plants that live in dry places may have long roots. They grow down to find water in the ground.

Plants that live in wet places may have roots above the ground. That way, the plant does not get too much water.

roots

▲ **The banyan tree lives in a wet place. Its roots grow above the ground.**

Roots also help animals. Bears, raccoons, and porcupines are some of the animals that eat roots.

We eat roots, too. Radishes, carrots, and beets are some of the roots we eat.

carrots

beets

✔ Quick Check

Circle the answers.

3. Plants that live in dry places may have _____ roots.

   short   long   thick

4. We eat roots, such as carrots and _____.

   apples   roses   beets

What do flowers, fruit, and seeds do?

Many plants have flowers. **Flowers** are the parts of plants that make seeds.

Inside a flower is a sticky powder called **pollen**. Pollen helps flowers make seeds.

flowers

▲ We eat the flowers of the broccoli plant.

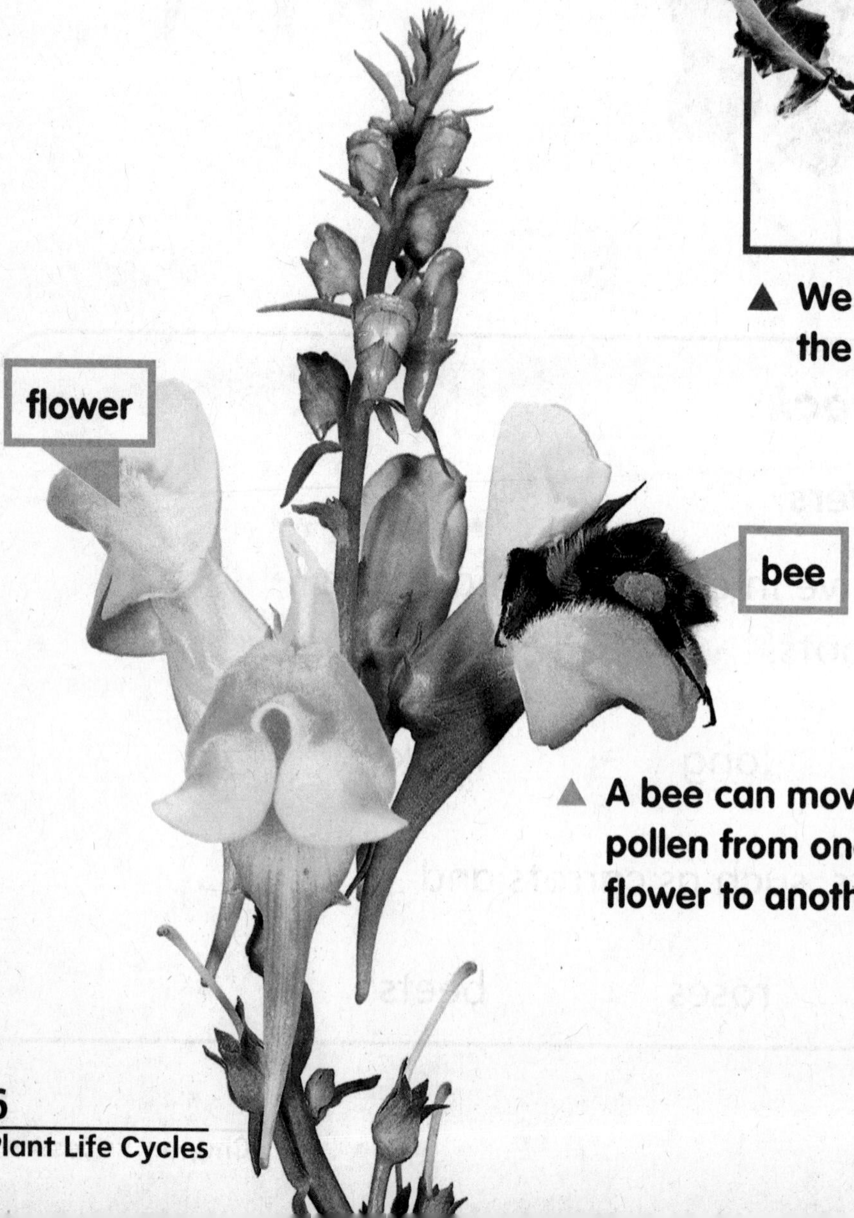

flower

bee

▲ A bee can move pollen from one flower to another.

Plants that have flowers make fruit.
Most of the time, seeds grow inside a fruit.
The **fruit** keeps the seeds safe and helps
them grow. The **seeds** can grow into new
plants. We eat the fruits of many plants,
such as apples.

apple

seeds

✔ Quick Check

5. Draw a picture of one of your favorite fruits.
Label your picture.

How do flowers make seeds?

One part of the flower makes pollen. Another part of the flower uses the pollen to make seeds. The seeds can grow into new plants.

Cantaloupe

from here

to here

1. Pollen moves from one part of the flower to another.

2. The flower grows bigger and the petals fall off. It grows into a fruit.

3. The fruit protects the seeds inside.

Read a Diagram

Animals, such as birds and bees, can move pollen from one part of a flower to another. Wind and water can move pollen, too.

4. When the fruit is ripe, it is ready to eat.

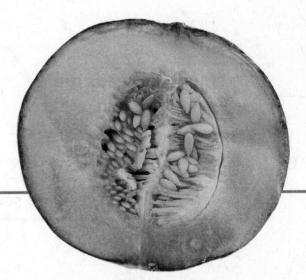

5. The seeds inside the fruit can grow into new plants.

 Quick Check

Fill in the blanks.

6. After a flower's petals fall off, it grows into a

_____.

7. A fruit's seeds can grow into new

_____.

How do seeds look?

Seeds have many different shapes and sizes. They all need light, water, and food to grow.

Marigold seeds are small and thin. ▶

marigold seeds

marigold

star anise

star anise pod

▲ A pod is a shell for seeds. This pod has room for many seeds.

All seeds have covers that protect them. The covers also help keep the seeds from drying out. Some seeds, like peanuts, also have shells.

▲ Peanuts are seeds. They grow underground.

The peanut shell is hard and light brown.

The cover of a peanut seed is thin and dark brown.

✔ Quick Check

Circle the answers.

8. A pod is a _____ for seeds.

   cover   shell

9. A peanut shell is light brown and _____.

   hard   soft

How do seeds move?

Animals help move seeds to new places. Many animals eat fruit and leave the seeds behind. Some animals, like squirrels, bury seeds. Some seeds stick to an animal's fur and move to new places.

▲ **This young baboon eats fruit with seeds.**

▲ **This bison carries seeds on its fur.**

Oceans and rivers can move seeds, too. Seeds fall into the water and are carried to new places. Wind can also carry seeds far away.

 The wind can carry this maple tree seed to a different place. ▶

✓ **Quick Check**

Complete the web. Tell other ways that seeds move.

10.

How Seeds Move

wind

How are plants like their parents?

You know that animals have babies that look and act like their parents. Plants are the same way.

A sunflower makes seeds that grow into sunflowers. An oak tree makes acorns that grow into oak trees.

sunflower

sunflower seed

acorn

oak tree

Most young plants look like their parent plants. Their flowers, petals, and leaves will have the same shape. Some plants, like tulips, may look a little different from their parent plants.

▲ **Tulips come in different colors.**

Quick Check

II. What do sunflower seeds grow up to be?

_____

12. How are young plants like their parents?

_____

What is a life cycle?

A **life cycle** shows how a living thing grows, changes, and makes new living things. The plant life cycle begins with a seed. It keeps going as plants make new plants.

Life Cycle of a Pine Tree

1. Pine trees make seeds inside cones.

2. The cones fall to the ground. Some seeds get moved to new places.

3. A seed becomes a young plant.

4. The young plant grows bigger. It grows cones that become new plants.

Read a Diagram

What does a pine tree make instead of flowers?

Science in Motion Watch a plant grow @ **www.macmillanmh.com**

Plants follow the same life cycles as their parent plants. Different plants have different life cycles. Some plants live for a few weeks. Others live for many years.

▲ These flowers go through their life cycle in a few months.

▲ Redwood trees take more than two years to make cones.

✔ Quick Check

Circle the answers.

13. The plant life cycle begins with a seed.

    true   false

14. Plants have the same life cycle as the parent plant.

    true   false

How can plants change to get what they need?

Plants need light to grow. Plant parts can move to get the light they need. The stems and leaves can bend toward the light. Flowers can turn toward the light, too.

▲ **This plant bends toward the light that comes through the window.**

▲ **Some flowers turn to face the Sun as it moves across the sky.**

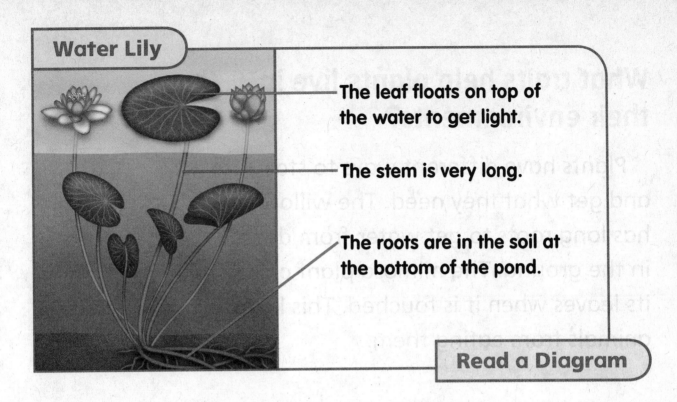

Water Lily

The leaf floats on top of the water to get light.

The stem is very long.

The roots are in the soil at the bottom of the pond.

Read a Diagram

Plants need soil to grow. They take in nutrients and water from the soil. The roots of a water lily grow down in the soil. The stem grows up toward the light.

✓ Quick Check

Circle the answers.

15. The _____ and _____ can turn to get light.

   flowers   roots   leaves

16. A water lily's stem is very _____.

   short   thick   long

What traits help plants live in their environments?

Plants have different ways to stay safe and get what they need. The willow tree has long roots to get water from deep in the ground. The mimosa plant closes its leaves when it is touched. This keeps animals from eating them.

▲ The leaves of this mimosa plant are open.

▲ The leaves of this mimosa plant are closed.

The weather causes some plants to change the way they grow.

▲ **This tree is growing to one side because of strong winds.**

 **Quick Check**

Fill in the blanks.

17. A willow tree has long _____.

18. A mimosa plant _____ its leaves when it is touched.

Draw a line from each word to its definition.

 flowers

 fruit

 life cycle

 pollen

 seeds

1. Parts of plants that grow into new plants.

2. A sticky powder inside flowers.

3. A plant part that keeps seeds safe.

4. Parts of plants that make seeds.

5. Steps that show how a living thing grows.

CHAPTER 2

Animal Life Cycles

The Big Idea How do animals grow and change?

Vocabulary

classify group things that are alike

mammals animals that have hair or fur and feed their young milk

reptiles animals that have scales and are cold-blooded

larva a young animal that hatches from an egg and looks different from its parents

pupa what a larva becomes when it forms a hard cover around its body

population a group of the same kind of animal living near each other

How do we classify animals?

When you **classify**, you group animals or things that are alike. Scientists classify animals into several groups. In some groups, animals have backbones. In some groups, animals do not have backbones.

hawk

grasshopper

trout

worm

Which of these animals do you think have backbones?

Touch the back of your neck. Do you feel bumps? They are part of your backbone. Your backbone goes from your hips all the way up to your head.

Squirrel Backbone

Read a Diagram

 Quick Check

Fill in the blanks.

I. Some animals do not have

_____.

2. A squirrel's backbone goes from its head to its

_____.

How can we classify animals with backbones?

Scientists classify animals with backbones into smaller groups, such as mammals, reptiles, birds, and fish.

Mammals are warm-blooded animals that have hair or fur. **Reptiles** are cold-blooded animals that have scales.

alligator

▲ Most reptiles, like the alligator, lay eggs.

lions

▲ Mammals give birth to their young.

Birds are the only animals with feathers. But not all birds can fly. Fish live in water. They breathe with body parts called gills.

bluebird

A bluebird is a bird that can fly. ▶

salmon

gills

▲ Fish have fins that help them swim.

✔ Quick Check

3. List four animal groups with backbones.

_____

4. What group of animals has feathers?

_____

How can we classify animals without backbones?

There are many kinds of animals that do not have backbones. Some of these animals have shells or hard body coverings that help keep them safe.

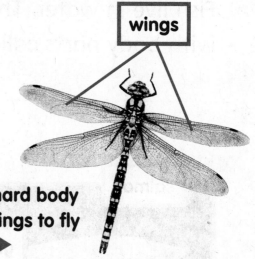
wings

The dragonfly has a hard body covering. It uses its wings to fly away from enemies. ▶

claws

▲ The lobster has a hard body covering. It uses its claws to break open food.

legs

The beetle has a hard shell. It has three body parts and six legs. ▶

Some animals without backbones do not have shells. They have soft bodies. These animals must use other ways to stay safe.

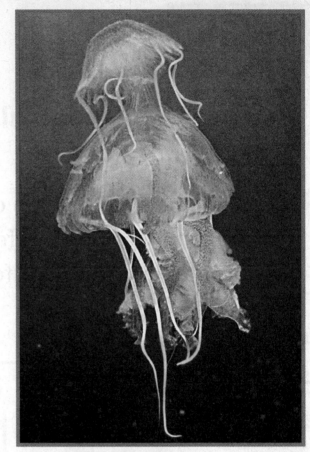

These jellyfish do not have shells. They sting other animals to stay safe. ▶

 Quick Check

Write about two ways that animals without backbones can stay safe.

5. _____

_____

_____

How does a mammal grow and change?

All animals go through a life cycle, just like plants. Different kinds of animals have different life cycles.

Panda Life Cycle

1. When a baby panda is born, its mother feeds it and keeps it safe.

2. A panda cub likes to climb and play. But it still needs its mother to find food and stay safe.

3. An adult panda can find its own food. It can have its own babies. If it does, the life cycle begins again.

Read a Diagram

When mammals are born, they need their mothers to live. The babies get milk from their mothers. Then they grow up and change into adults.

A mother panda keeps her cub safe. ▶

 Quick Check

Write *true* if the sentence is true. Write *false* if the sentence is false.

6. All animals have the same life cycle.

_____

7. Baby mammals need help to stay safe.

_____

8. An adult panda cannot find its own food.

_____

How are baby animals and their parents alike and different?

Baby animals can look and act like their parents. Sea lion pups have a tail, flippers, and fur like their parents. They swim and eat fish like their parents.

◀ **California sea lions**

Baby animals can look different from their parents in some ways. This cat gave birth to three kittens. The kittens look different from their mother. The kittens look different from one another, too.

How are the kittens like their mother? How are they different? ▶

✓ Quick Check

9. Draw a baby animal and its mother. Show how they are alike and different.

Why do animals lay many eggs?

Birds, reptiles, and fish lay eggs. Insects and many kinds of sea animals lay eggs, too. Animals lay many eggs because some of the young animals will not live. Many young animals get eaten by other animals.

▲ A queen bee can lay more than 2,000 eggs in one day.

salmon

Salmon also lay thousands of eggs. They lay their eggs in between rocks in rivers. ▶

Many animals that lay eggs do not care for their young. Female sea turtles bury their eggs in the sand and leave.

When the eggs hatch, the baby turtles must find their own way to the ocean. Many young turtles get eaten by other animals, such as seagulls.

Sometimes people protect baby sea turtles from animals that will eat them. ▶

✓ Quick Check

Circle the answers.

10. Birds, reptiles, and _____ lay eggs.

    lions   mammals   fish

11. Sometimes _____ try to help sea turtles.

    people   seagulls   mother turtles

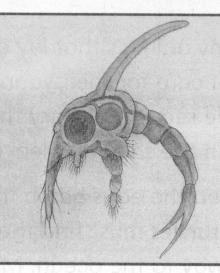

1. The adult female crab lays many eggs in a spongy clump.

2. After two weeks, the eggs hatch. A crab larva comes out of the egg. The larva looks different from its parents.

How do animals from eggs become adults?

Most eggs have an outside shell. It keeps the animal growing inside safe. After the animal is fully formed, it hatches from the egg.

The animal grows bigger and becomes an adult. Then it can have its own young, and the life cycle begins again.

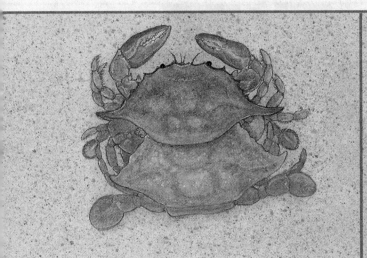

3. After five weeks, the young crab sheds, or loses, its shell so it can grow bigger.

4. As the crab grows, it keeps on shedding its shell. After about 16 months, it becomes an adult and can lay eggs of its own.

Read a Diagram

 Quick Check

Fill in the blanks.

12. Most eggs have an outside covering or

_____.

13. A larva looks _____
from its parents.

1. Butterflies lay their eggs on leaves or branches.

2. After ten days, the egg hatches and a caterpillar comes out. The caterpillar is a larva. The larva eats leaves and grows.

How does a butterfly grow and change?

Butterflies begin life looking very different from their parents. They go through four steps, or stages, as they grow into adults.

3. After three weeks, the caterpillar spins a thread and attaches itself to a branch. Now it is a pupa. Inside a hard case, the pupa changes into a butterfly.

4. When the butterfly is fully grown, it crawls out of the hard case.

5. The butterfly is ready to fly and lay eggs of its own.

 Quick Check

14. When does a butterfly not look like its parent?

_____

15. What happens to the pupa?

_____

How do traits help animals?

All animals look and act in special ways that help them live. Sometimes their color or their body parts help them. Sometimes the things they do can help them.

▲ Male peacocks have bright feathers and sing loud songs that help females find them.

▲ Giraffes have long necks that help them eat leaves in tall trees.

Animals do things to stay safe, too. Some animals fly away when they are in danger. Other animals blend into their surroundings or fight. The bites of some snakes and spiders are poisonous.

Tortoise

Read a Photo

 Quick Check

Tell how each animal stays safe.

16. tortoise _____ .

17. bird _____ .

18. snake _____ .

What is a population?

A **population** is a group of the same kind of animal living near each other. For example, the black bears that live in Yosemite National Park are one population. The black bears that live in Maine are another population.

▲ **Black bears with black fur are found in Maine.**

Animals in different populations do not always look the same. In order to live safely in different places, animals can change in many ways.

▲ Do not be fooled by the name! The black bears that live in Yosemite National Park have brown fur.

▲ Some black bears in Alaska have light fur that helps them hide in the snow.

 Quick Check

Write *true* if the sentence is true. Write *false* if the sentence is false.

19. Black bears live in different parts of the

United States. _____

20. All black bears have black fur. _____

How can we compare animals in the same population?

Animals in the same population may look and act in different ways. For example, meerkats are animals that live in the African desert. Some meerkats are bigger than others. Some are more careful. Others are more curious.

meerkats

Meerkats are also alike in many ways. They all eat insects and live underground in burrows. They have long claws for digging and live in large groups.

◄ **This meerkat is digging to find insects to eat.**

 Quick Check

Complete each sentence by writing a fact about meerkats.

21. Some meerkats _____ .

22. All meerkats _____ .

Draw a line from each word to its definition.

classify

population

larva

pupa

mammals

reptiles

I. A group of the same kind of animal living near each other.

2. A young animal that hatches from an egg and looks different from its parents.

3. Animals with hair or fur that feed their young milk.

4. To group things that are alike.

5. What a larva becomes when it forms a hard cover around itself.

6. Cold-blooded animals that have scales.

CHAPTER 3

Earth's Minerals

How can we describe rocks and soil?

Vocabulary

geologist a scientist who studies rocks and puts them into groups	
minerals what rocks are made of	
property tells you something about an object—for example, its color	
luster how a mineral looks when light shines on it	
hardness how tough a mineral is	
weathering the way water and wind change rocks	
soil made up of tiny rocks and bits of plants and animals	

How can we describe rocks?

A **geologist** is a scientist who studies rocks. One thing geologists look at is a rock's color.

Many rocks are one color. Others are more than one color. Most rocks are gray. But some rocks are black, brown, red, white, or pink.

| gabbro | basalt | chalk | obsidian |

| ironstone | pink granite | mudstone | shale |

Geologists look at the size of rocks, too. Rocks that are the same size might not weigh the same.

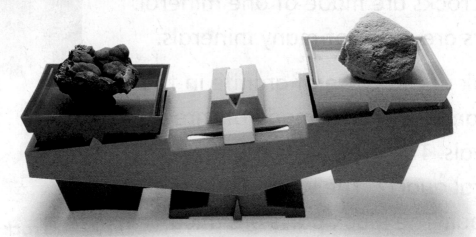

▲ These two rocks are the same size. But the rock on the right weighs less than the rock on the left.

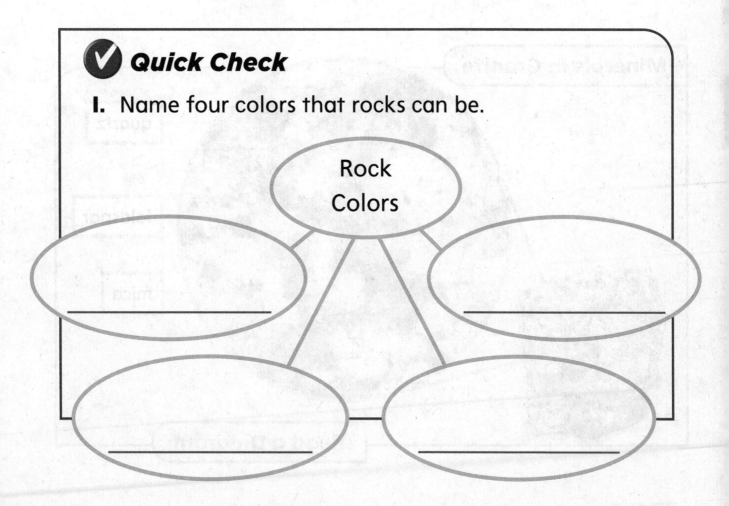

✅ Quick Check

1. Name four colors that rocks can be.

Rock Colors

What are rocks made of?

All rocks are made of **minerals**. Some rocks are made of one mineral. Others are made of many minerals.

Look at the piece of granite in the diagram below. It is made of three minerals. The gray parts are the mineral quartz. The white parts are feldspar. The black parts are mica.

▲ This rock is called beryl. It is made of only one mineral.

Minerals in Granite

quartz

feldspar

mica

Read a Diagram

Did you know that you use minerals every day? A pencil lead is made of the mineral graphite. Our bodies need minerals, too. We get minerals from the foods we eat. Even our toothpaste has a mineral.

fluorite

fluorite mine

 Many toothpastes have fluoride, which is made from the mineral, fluorite.

✔ Quick Check

Fill in the blanks.

2. Granite is made of three _____.

3. The mineral in a pencil is _____.

How can we describe minerals?

A **property** tells you something about an object. Color is one property of a mineral. Luster is another property. **Luster** tells how a mineral looks when light shines on it.

▲ Pyrite's luster and color make it look like gold.

▲ Some minerals, like quartz, shine like glass.

▲ The mineral halloysite does not shine. It has a dull luster.

Another property of a mineral is its hardness. **Hardness** is how tough a mineral is.

Talc is a soft mineral. You can scratch it with your fingernail. Diamond is a hard mineral. It can only be cut by another diamond.

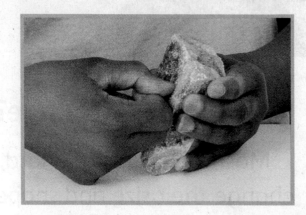

▲ Talc is the softest mineral.

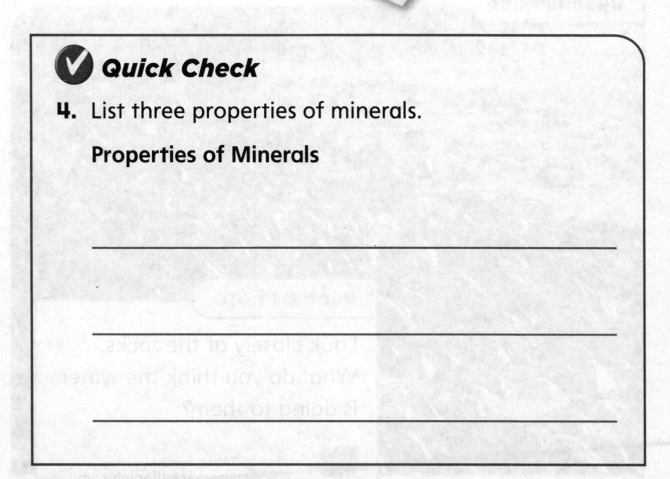

◄ Diamond is the hardest mineral.

✓ Quick Check

4. List three properties of minerals.

Properties of Minerals

_____

_____

_____

How do rocks change?

Most rocks are very hard, but they can change their size and shape. **Weathering** is the way water and wind change rocks.

When water gets into the cracks of rocks, it can freeze and push against the rocks. Then the cracks get bigger and the rocks break.

Beach Rocks

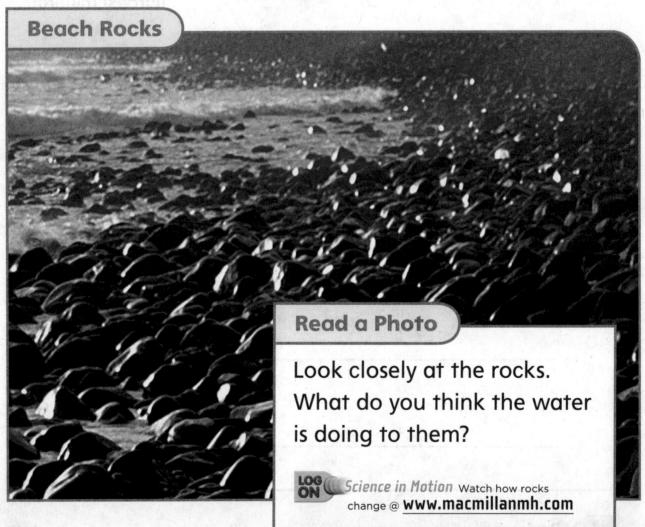

Read a Photo

Look closely at the rocks. What do you think the water is doing to them?

LOG ON *Science in Motion* Watch how rocks change @ **www.macmillanmh.com**

 Strong winds can blow sand against rocks. Wind and sand made a hole in this rock.

▲ When rocks slide down a hill, they may break and become smaller.

✔ Quick Check

Write *true* if the sentence is true. Write *false* if the sentence is false.

5. Rocks can change their size. _____

6. Water can make rocks break. _____

7. When rocks slide down a hill, they get larger.

_____

In what other ways can rocks change?

Earthquakes can change rocks, too. In an earthquake, rocks rub against each other and break into smaller pieces.

Plants can also change rocks. Plants can grow in soil inside the cracks of rocks. Sometimes a plant's roots are so strong they cause the rocks to break.

The roots of this tree have grown into the rock and cracked it. ▶

You know that rocks are made of minerals. Water can cause some minerals to change.

▲ Water caused the iron in this rock to rust and turn red and brown.

▲ Water caused the copper in this rock to turn green.

✔ Quick Check

8. Draw a picture that shows one way a rock can change. Label your picture and write a sentence about it.

What is in soil?

Soil is made up of tiny rocks and bits of plants and animals. Weathering makes large rocks break down into smaller rocks. They become part of the soil. When plants and animals die, they also break down and become part of the soil.

Soil

leaf

snail

rock

Read a Diagram

Most plants grow in soil. Plants grow by taking in minerals from the soil. People need minerals to grow, too. One way we get minerals is by eating plants.

Plants get minerals from the soil. Then people get minerals from eating plants. ▶

✔ Quick Check

9. Name three things that are part of soil.

_____

10. How can people get the minerals they need?

_____

What are some kinds of soil?

Did you know there are different kinds of soil? The minerals in the rocks give these soils their color.

clay soil

▲ Red clay soil gets its color from tiny pieces of iron. It does not hold much water.

sandy soil

▲ Sandy soil is light brown and does not hold much water.

Most plants grow best in topsoil. Plants that do not need much water grow best in sandy soil. Some plants grow best in a mix of topsoil and sandy soil.

topsoil

▲ Topsoil is dark brown or black and can hold lots of water. It has bits of dead animals and plants in it.

✓ Quick Check

Circle the answer.

II. The color of red soil comes from _____ .

iron   plants   animals

I2. Most plants grow best in _____ .

sandy soil   clay soil   topsoil

How do animals help the soil?

Ants, worms, rabbits, and gophers live underground. They dig tunnels in the soil. The digging mixes the soil. This helps air and water get into the soil. The air and water help plants grow.

When animals die, their bodies break down and become part of the soil. This makes the soil healthy and helps new plants to grow.

▲ Gophers dig tunnels and mix the soil.

✔ Quick Check

13. List three types of soil.

_____

_____

14. Write about two ways animals help soil.

_____

_____

Complete each sentence with words from the box.

geologist	hardness	luster	minerals
property	soil	weathering	

1. All rocks are made of _____ .

2. Rocks are changed by _____ .

3. A scientist who studies rocks is a _____ .

4. Color is an example of a _____ .

5. Two properties of minerals are _____

and _____ .

6. Tiny rocks are found in _____ .

CHAPTER 4

Earth's Past

The Big Idea

What can fossils tell us about Earth's past?

Vocabulary

fossil what is left of a living thing from the past

paleontologist a scientist who studies fossils

extinct a living thing that has died out and has none of its kind living on Earth

skeleton an animal's full set of bones

What are fossils?

A **fossil** is what is left of a living thing from the past. Some fossils are bones or teeth of animals that lived long ago. Other fossils are prints of plants or animals. Fossils help us see what life was like long ago.

▲ **These dinosaur eggs were found in China.**

◀ **A fern left a print in this rock.**

Some fossils of plants and animals are found in rock. Others are found in ice, tar, or amber. Amber is a sticky liquid in trees that has become hard. Sometimes plants or insects got trapped in amber and became fossils.

▲ This insect got trapped in amber millions of years ago.

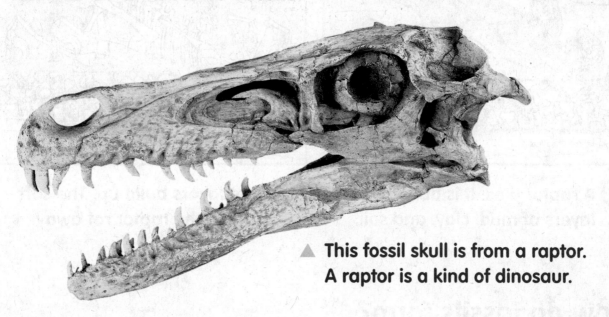

▲ This fossil skull is from a raptor. A raptor is a kind of dinosaur.

✔ Quick Check

1. Name two kinds of fossils.

_____ and _____.

2. Name two places where fossils can be found.

_____ and _____.

How a Fossil Forms

① A raptor dies. It is buried in layers of mud, clay, and soil.

② More layers build up. The soft parts of the raptor rot away.

How do fossils form?

Fossils form when living things are buried under many layers of sand or mud. Scientists can tell how old a fossil is by looking at the layers. Fossils in the same layer are from plants or animals that lived at about the same time.

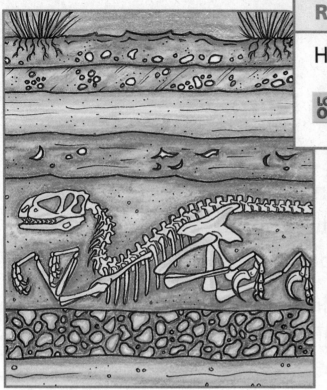

Read a Diagram

How does the fossil form?

LOG ON *Science in Motion* Watch how fossils form @ **www.macmillanmh.com**

 3 The bones and teeth slowly harden into rock.

4 Millions of years later, the fossil is found.

✓ Quick Check

Fill in the blanks.

3. Fossils are buried under many

_____ of soil.

4. Fossils that are found in the same layer

_____ at about the same time.

How can fossils help us learn about the past?

A **paleontologist** is a scientist who studies fossils. Fossils give clues about what Earth was like long ago.

Animal fossils tell what kinds of animals lived on Earth. They also tell what the land might have looked like.

A paleontologist found this fish fossil in a dry place in Wyoming. What do you think this place was like long ago?

In Antarctica paleontologists have found plant fossils under the ice. These fossils look like plants that grow in warm places today. That means that the weather in Antarctica used to be warm.

Palm Leaf Fossil

Antarctica

Read a Photo

✓ Quick Check

5. What does a paleontologist do?

_____

6. What does the palm leaf fossil tell you about Antarctica?

_____

What can fossils teach us about extinct animals?

When a living thing is **extinct**, it has died out. None of its kind lives anywhere on Earth.

Some plants and animals become extinct because of disease. Sometimes big changes on Earth cause plants and animals to die out.

▲ **The head of this mammoth, an extinct animal, was found in the ice.**

Paleontologists use fossils to learn about extinct animals. First they find fossil bones. Then they put them together to make a **skeleton**. A skeleton is a full set of bones. This helps them learn about the animal's size and how it might have moved.

▲ This scientist is cleaning the mammoth fossil.

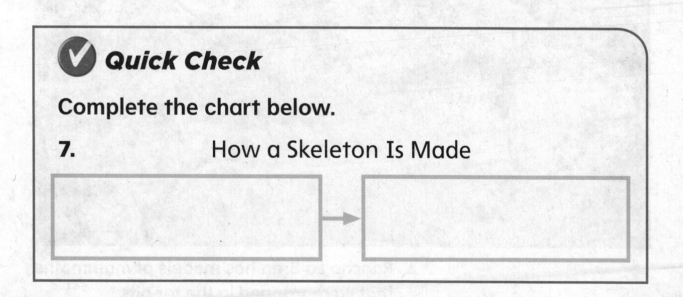

✓ Quick Check

Complete the chart below.

7. How a Skeleton Is Made

What are the La Brea Tar Pits?

At Rancho La Brea in California, thick asphalt comes up from the Earth. The asphalt is black and sticky like tar. Paleontologists have found about 3 million plant and animal fossils in the pits. Some of them are about 40,000 years old.

▲ Rancho La Brea has models of mammoths that were trapped in the tar pits.

Scientists think the weather used to be warm and humid because they found fossils of frogs and turtles. They also found fossils of leaves, cones, and seeds. Today, asphalt still traps plants and animals in the pits. Some will become fossils many years from now.

▲ **This paleontologist is taking fossils out of the tar pits.**

 Quick Check

Write **true** if the sentence is true. Write **false** if the sentence is false.

8. The asphalt at Rancho La Brea is like tar.

_____

9. Millions of fossils have been found at

Rancho La Brea. _____

10. Scientists think the weather there used to

be cold. _____

What other fossils are found in California?

The Ankylosaur was covered with bony plates. It lived about 100 million years ago. Its fossils were found in Carlsbad, California. It ate plants.

Ankylosaur

The Lambeosaurus was a dinosaur that lived 76 million years ago. Its fossils were found in Baja California, a part of Mexico. It ate plants with its flat teeth.

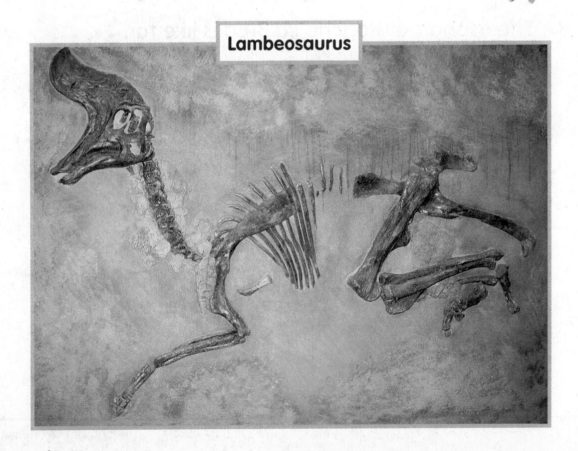

Lambeosaurus

Another kind of fossil is petrified wood. When dead trees are covered by water, mud, and ash they slowly turn to stone. Scientists can count the rings in petrified wood to tell how old it was when it died.

▲ Petrified wood is found in many parts of California.

✔ Quick Check

Fill in the blanks.

II. The Lambeosaurus and Ankylosaur were

dinosaurs that ate _____.

I2. Petrified wood is another kind of

_____ .

Circle the correct answer.

1. A paleontologist is a scientist who studies _____ .

weather   flowers   fossils

2. An example of an animal that is extinct is a _____ .

skeleton   dinosaur   geologist

3. A fossil is what is left of a living thing from the _____ .

present   past   future

4. A skeleton is an animal's full set of _____ .

bones   teeth   paws

CHAPTER 5

Earth's Resources

How do we use Earth's resources?

Vocabulary

natural resource something from Earth that people use

fuel something that gives off heat when it burns

solar power using sunlight to make electric power

What are natural resources?

A **natural resource** is something from Earth that people use. Rocks, minerals, plants, soil, and water are natural resources. We use natural resources to make things we use every day.

▲ **People use things from nature to live.**

Some shirts are made of cotton. Cotton comes from a plant. Your desk might be made of wood. Wood comes from a tree. Look at the diagram below. It shows what we use to make a pencil.

Pencil

The eraser is made from liquid inside a rubber tree.

The yellow part of this pencil is made of wood.

The gray part is made of graphite, a mineral.

Read a Diagram

✓ Quick Check

1. What are three examples of natural resources?

_____

2. Which parts of a pencil come from a tree?

_____

How do we use rocks and soil?

Rocks and soil are natural resources. We need rocks and soil to live. Rocks break down and become part of the soil. Plants use the soil to grow. We use plants for food and for making things, such as paper and clothing.

▲ **The corn plants need rocks and soil to grow.**

We use rocks in other ways. We make concrete by mixing rocks, sand, and water. Concrete is used to make buildings and sidewalks. We use the minerals in sand to make glass.

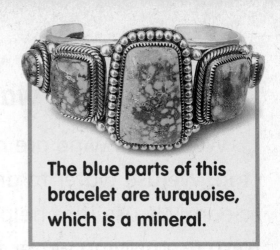

The blue parts of this bracelet are turquoise, which is a mineral.

◄ This building was made with rocks.

✔ Quick Check

Circle the answer.

3. Plants are used to make clothing.

    true   false

4. Concrete is made from rocks, sand, and water.

    true   false

5. Buildings can be made from rocks.

    true   false

How do we use water and wind?

Water and wind are natural resources, too. We use water to drink, cook, and clean. We use it to help plants grow. We also use moving water to make electric power. Electric power lights up and heats our homes.

The machines inside the dam make electric power. ▶

▲ **The water moves over the dam very quickly.**

Have you ever seen a sailboat move across the water or a flag wave in the wind? Then you know that wind can make things move. Wind can also be used to make electric power, just like water.

▲ These windmills are used to make electric power.

✓ Quick Check

Fill in the blanks.

6. We use water to drink, cook, and _____.

7. When water and wind move, they can make

_____ power.

How do we use plants?

Many plants are used for food. Fruits, vegetables, and seeds come from plants. The seeds of some plants are called grains. Grains can be ground, or crushed, into flour. The flour is then used to make cereal and bread.

From Wheat to Bread

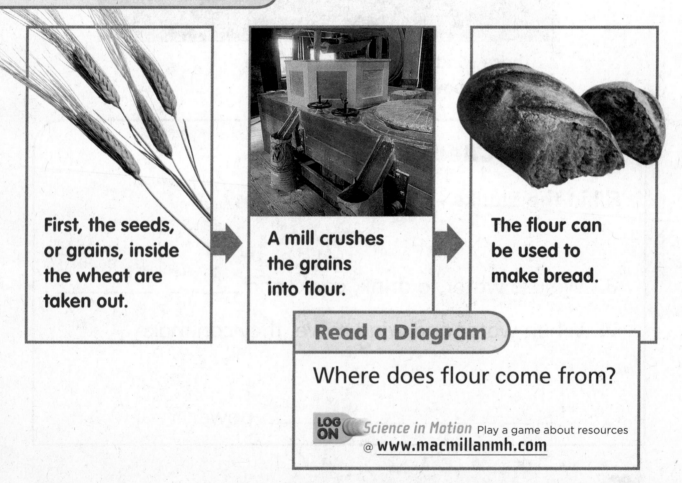

First, the seeds, or grains, inside the wheat are taken out.

A mill crushes the grains into flour.

The flour can be used to make bread.

Read a Diagram

Where does flour come from?

LOG ON *Science in Motion* Play a game about resources @ **www.macmillanmh.com**

We use plants in many other ways. Some rugs and clothes are made from cotton plants. We use wood from trees to make buildings, furniture, and paper.

cotton

▲ Cotton is used to make clothes.

aloe

▲ A liquid inside aloe leaves helps heal burns.

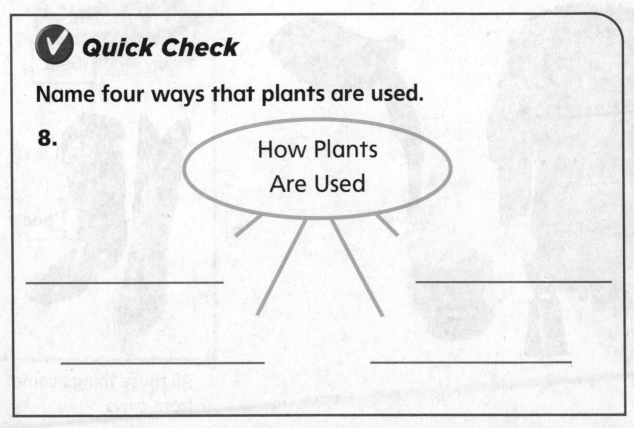

✔ Quick Check

Name four ways that plants are used.

8.

How Plants Are Used

How do people use animals?

Animals are natural resources, too. Many people eat chicken, fish, and other animals. The milk from cows, goats, and sheep is used to make butter and cheese.

Leather is made from animal skins. Shoes and coats can be made from leather.

milk

cheese

beef

boots

▲ All these things come from cows.

A **fuel** is something that gives off heat when it burns. We burn wood to give us heat. We also burn coal and oil.

Long ago, coal and oil formed underground from dead plants and animals. Now we use coal and oil to cook and heat our homes.

Gasoline is a fuel made from oil. Cars and trucks burn gasoline to move. ▶

✓ Quick Check

Circle the answer.

9. We get milk from cows, sheep, and _____.

fish   goats   pigs

10. A fuel that we put in cars is _____.

gasoline   wood   coal

How does California get energy?

People in California use water, wind, and oil to make electric power. They also use **solar power**, which is energy from the Sun. Special machines, called solar panels, change sunlight into electric power.

Solar Power

Read a Photo

In California, there is natural gas under the ground. Workers find it and send it through pipes to buildings. Natural gas can be burned to heat buildings and cook food.

▲ These people are cooking with natural gas.

✓ *Quick Check*

11. What do solar panels use to make electric power?

_____

12. How do people use natural gas?

_____

What are other natural resources in California?

California is sunny and warm. The soil is filled with minerals. Farmers grow many different crops, such as avocados, walnuts, grapes and oranges. People in all parts of the United States eat fruits and vegetables from the Golden State.

▲ **Strawberries grow well in California.**

California has many other natural resources. People dig for gravel, clay, silver, and gold. In the 1800s, many people came to California to look for gold. Today, gold can still be found in California.

gold nugget

◀ **This old photograph shows people digging for gold in the 1800s.**

 Quick Check

Fill in the blanks.

13. California's _____ is filled with minerals.

14. People dig for natural resources, such as gold, silver,

gravel, and _____ .

Write the word or words in the box under
the correct meaning.

| fuel | natural resource | solar power |

1. It is a way of using sunlight to make power.

_____

2. It gives off heat when it burns.

_____

3. It is something from Earth that people use.

_____

CHAPTER 6

Objects in Motion

 How do things move?

Vocabulary

position the place where something is

distance how far away one thing is from another

motion when something moves or changes position

speed how far something moves in a certain amount of time

force what is done to move something

push move something away from you

pull move something closer to you

friction a force that slows down moving things

How can you describe where something is?

Position is the place where something is. You can describe the position of an object by comparing it to something that does not move. You can use words such as in, on, under, next to, left, right, above, below, near, and far to describe position.

The orange fish is to the left of the chest.

When something moves, it changes its position. You can describe its new position by comparing it to other objects.

Where is the orange fish now?
How did it move?

**Quick Check**

I. Draw a picture of many objects. Write a sentence about the position of one object.

How do you measure distance?

Distance is how far away one thing is from another. There are different ways to measure distance. One way is by using a map.

California

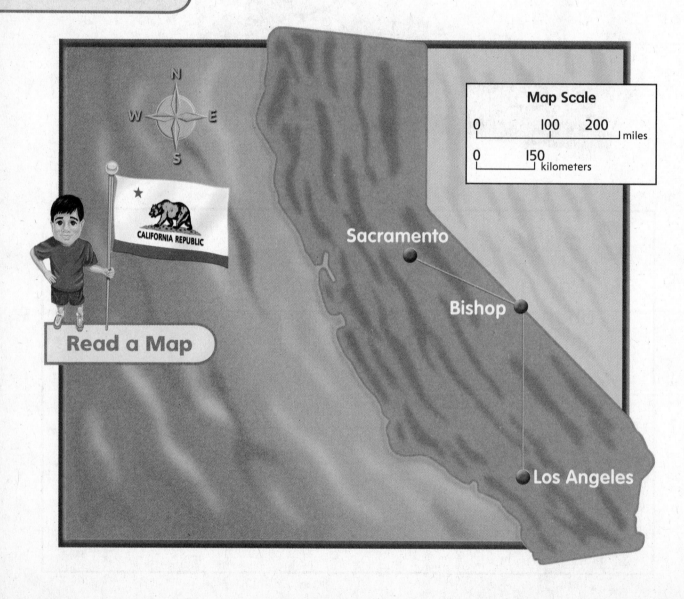

Read a Map

Map Scale

0   100   200
| | miles

0   150
| | kilometers

Sacramento

Bishop

Los Angeles

You can use units, such as inches, feet, and miles to measure distance. You can also use metric units, such as centimeters, meters, and kilometers.

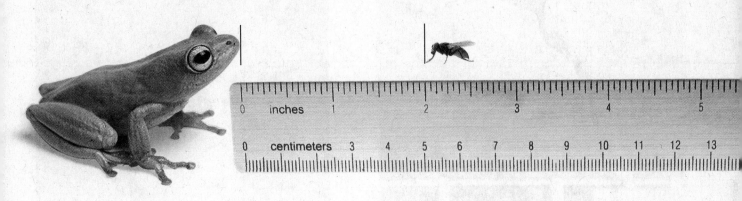

✔ Quick Check

2. Look at the map of California. Is it farther from Sacramento to Bishop or from Bishop to Los Angeles?

_____

3. Look at the photo of the frog and the fly.

How many inches away is the fly from the frog?

_____ How many centimeters? _____

How can you tell if something has moved?

All around you things move. **Motion** is a change in position. When something is moving, we say it is in motion. This diver is in motion. She starts at the top of a diving board. She jumps into the air and her body changes position.

As she prepares to enter the water, how has her position changed?

 Quick Check

Fill in the blanks.

4. When something moves, it starts in one

_____ and ends in another.

5. Something is in _____ when it is moving.

What is speed?

Speed is how far something moves in a certain amount of time. Have you ever watched a race? Most people can run half a mile in 5 minutes. But an Olympic runner can run I mile in just 5 minutes or less.

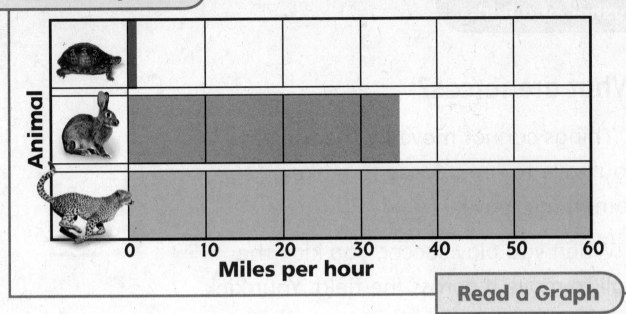

Read a Graph

✔ Quick Check

Write true if the sentence is true. Write false if the sentence is false.

6. Speed is how far something moves in a certain

amount of time. _____

7. The graph shows that the fastest animal is

the rabbit. _____

8. A turtle moves at less than 10 miles per hour.

_____

What are forces?

Things cannot move by themselves. You have to use a **force** to make something move.

When you play soccer, you kick the ball to move it across the field. Your kick is a force. If you did not kick the ball, it would stay in the same place.

Kicking

Read a Photo

If you **push** something, it moves away from you. A kick is a kind of push. If you **pull** something, it moves closer to you. When you open a drawer, you pull it toward yourself. A push or a pull is a force.

The man is pushing the man and boy in the wagon.

In this game, the children on each side of the rope are pulling it towards them.

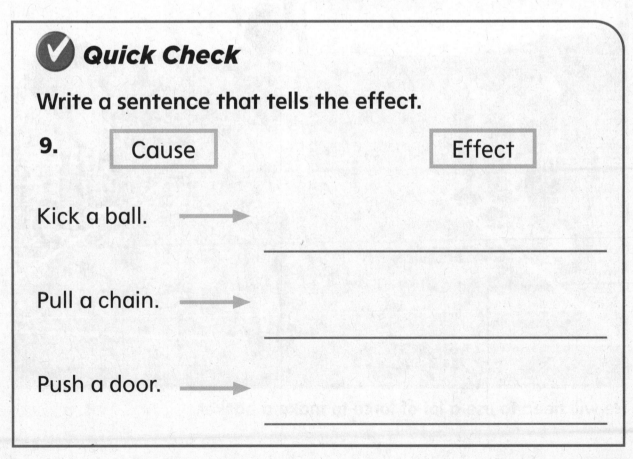

✓ Quick Check

Write a sentence that tells the effect.

9. | Cause | | Effect |

Kick a ball. ⟶ _____

Pull a chain. ⟶ _____

Push a door. ⟶ _____

What happens when a force changes?

When you use a lot of force to throw a ball, it goes far. When you toss a ball lightly, it will not go as far. If you use more force, things move faster and go further. If you use less force, things move slower and do not go as far.

He will need to use a lot of force to make a basket.

Light things are easier to move than heavy things. You use more force to move something heavy. Some objects are so heavy that people use handcarts, trucks or cranes to move them.

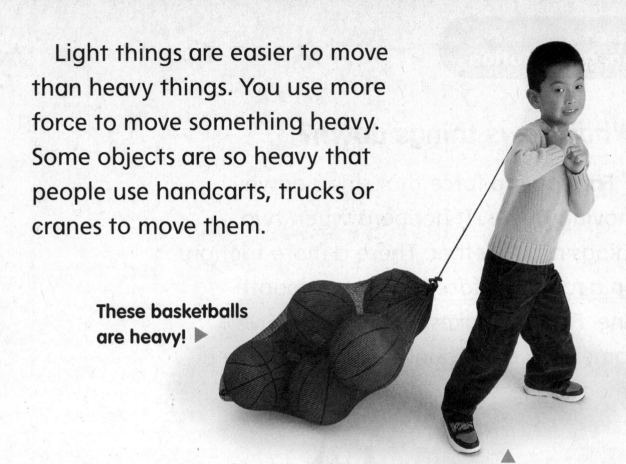

These basketballs are heavy! ▶

▲ **Pulling down on the string makes it easier to move the balls.**

✓ Quick Check

10. Draw a picture to show how you would move a heavy box. Write about the force you used.

What slows things down?

Friction is a force that slows down moving things. It happens when two things rub together. There is more friction on a rough surface than on a smooth one. Friction makes it harder to move something on a rough surface than on a smooth one.

To slow down, you drag a rubber stopper on the ground. The dragging causes friction.

Friction can be helpful. Running shoes have treads, or patterns, that add friction. This keeps runners from slipping and falling.

Other times, we try to have less friction. The bottoms of ballet slippers are smooth so dancers can slide easily across the floor.

The bottom of a surfboard is smooth so it can glide on the waves.

✓ Quick Check

Circle the answer.

11. There is more friction on a _____ surface.

smooth   shiny   rough

12. The treads on running shoes _____ friction.

add   subtract   stop

1. The pitcher uses force to throw the ball toward the batter.

2. The batter uses a push to hit the ball. It changes direction and flies toward the outfield.

How can forces change motion?

Forces can make things change motion. They can make things speed up, slow down, stop, and start moving. Forces can also make things change direction. In a softball game, the players use force to change the direction of a ball's motion.

3. The player in the field catches the ball. He stops its motion.

Read a Diagram

What kind of force do the players use?

 Science in Motion Watch forces at work
@ **www.macmillanmh.com**

✔ Quick Check

Fill in the blanks.

13. Forces can change the _____ of things.

14. In softball, the player that catches the ball

_____ its motion.

Use the clues to find the words. They go across and down.

1. how far away one thing is from another

2. what is needed to move something

3. when something changes position

4. a force that slows down moving things

5. the place where something is

6. move something closer to you

7. how far something moves in a certain amount of time

8. move something away from you

```
f  g  x  p  u  l  l  y  n
l  p  e  u  d  a  p  f  r
f  p  o  s  i  t  i  o  n
o  c  u  h  s  f  j  m  p
r  k  q  u  t  z  l  o  g
c  h  n  r  a  v  o  t  s
e  v  x  b  n  d  y  i  z
m  f  r  i  c  t  i  o  n
c  h  s  p  e  e  d  n  a
```

CHAPTER 7

Forces at Work

 What can forces do?

Vocabulary

simple machine a tool that makes the force of your push or pull stronger

lever a simple machine that lets you use less force to lift something

ramp a simple machine that helps you move things to a higher place

gravity a force that pulls things toward each other

weight the amount of force an object has

attract pull objects made of iron

poles the two parts of a magnet where its pull is the strongest

repel when the poles of two magnets push away from each other

sound a kind of energy you hear

vibrates moves back and forth in a fast way

What makes work easier?

A **simple machine** makes moving an object easier. It makes the force of your push or pull stronger. A **lever** is a simple machine that lets you use less force to lift something. Some examples of levers are forks, scissors, and seesaws.

▲ You can use a metal stick as a lever to open a can of paint.

A **ramp** is a simple machine that helps you move things to a higher place. A wheel is another simple machine that helps you move things. Wheels let you roll objects instead of lifting them.

▲ Pushing the box up a ramp is easier than lifting it up.

◄ The wheels on the stroller make it easier for the girl to push it.

✔ **Quick Check**

Fill in the blanks.

1. A fork is a _____ that moves food.

2. Using a _____ makes it easier to move things to a high place.

What is a tool?

A tool can be a simple machine, or it can be made up of many simple machines. A hammer is a tool that is one simple machine. An engine is a tool that is made up of many simple machines. All the parts work together to make a car move.

Egg Beater

Read a Photo

Look at these three tools.

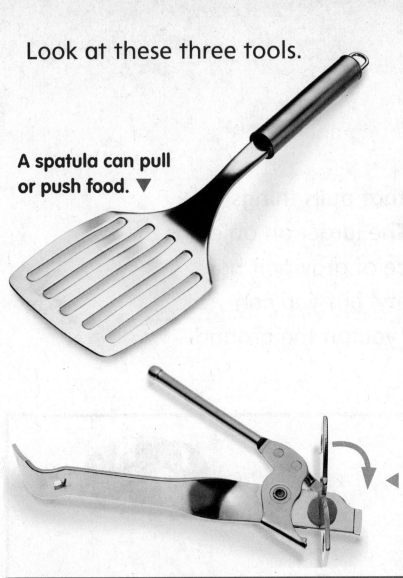

A spatula can pull or push food. ▼

▲ A nutcracker creates a force strong enough to break hard shells.

◀ Turning the can opener's sharp wheel can cut a metal lid.

✔ Quick Check

3. What does a hammer do?

_____

4. What does a spatula do?

_____

What is gravity?

Gravity is a force that pulls things toward each other. The larger an object is, the stronger the force of gravity it has. You cannot see gravity, but you can feel it. Gravity keeps you on the ground.

Gravity pulls the parachute toward Earth. ▲

Earth has a strong force of gravity because of its size. The gravity of Earth is stronger than the gravity of smaller things. That is why a ball in the air will fall back down to Earth.

Gravity at Work

Read a Diagram

Which has a stronger force of gravity, the ball or Earth?

LOG ON *Science in Motion* Watch this diagram in action @ **www.macmillanmh.com**

✓ *Quick Check*

Circle the answer.

5. Larger objects have a _____ force of gravity.

weaker   lighter   stronger

6. You cannot see gravity, but you can _____ it.

taste   feel   smell

What is weight?

Gravity pulls things toward the center of Earth with a certain amount of force. This amount of force is called **weight**. You can find out the weight of an object by putting it on a scale. A scale can measure weight in ounces, pounds, or even tons.

The guinea pig weighs about 2 pounds.
The pumpkin weighs about 7 pounds.

Planets and moons have more or less gravity than Earth. Our Moon is much smaller than Earth. That means it has less gravity than Earth. Things weigh less on the Moon than on Earth. If you weighed 60 pounds on Earth, you would weigh about 10 pounds on the Moon!

An astronaut can jump high on the Moon because there is less gravity to pull him down.

Quick Check

Write true if the sentence is true. Write false if the sentence is false.

7. A scale can measure the weight of an object.

_____

8. The Moon has more gravity than Earth.

_____

9. The Earth is larger than the Moon. _____

What does a magnet pull?

A magnet can **attract**, or pull, objects made of iron. A magnet will not attract a penny because it is not made of iron. Is a quarter made of iron? How could you find out?

This machine uses a very large magnet to pick up large objects made of iron.

Magnets can move things without even touching them. They can pull through solids like paper, plastic, or glass. They can pull through liquids and gases, too.

Magnets can pull metal objects through liquids and solids.

✔ Quick Check

Fill in the blanks.

10. A magnet attracts objects made of

_____.

11. Magnets can pull through solids, liquids, and

_____.

What are poles?

Magnets have two poles, a north pole and a south pole. The **poles** are where the pull of the magnet is the strongest.

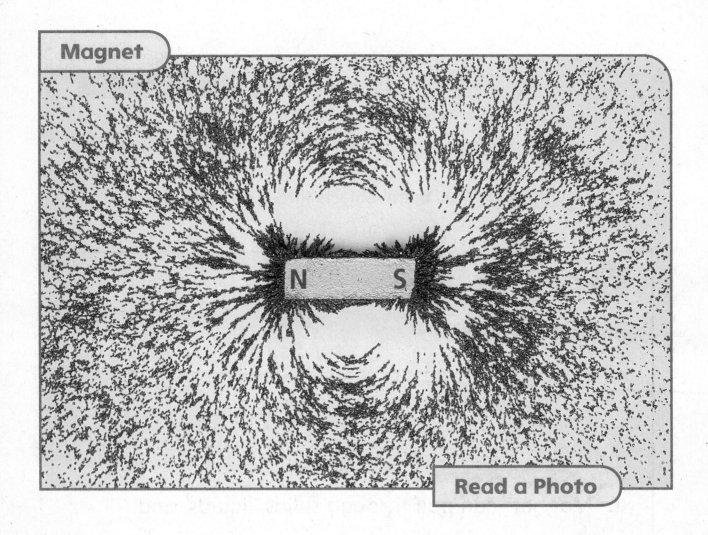

Magnet

N   S

Read a Photo

The poles of these magnets attract each other because they are opposites. A north pole and a south pole pull toward each other.

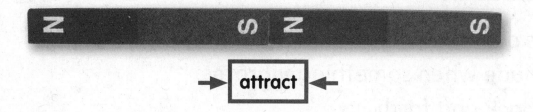

The poles of these magnets **repel**, or push away from each other. They repel each other because they are the same.

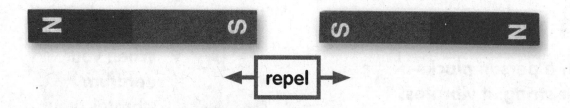

✔ Quick Check

12. What are the two poles of a magnet?

_____

13. When do the poles of two magnets repel each other?

_____

What is sound?

Sound is a kind of energy you hear.
Sound is made when something **vibrates**,
or moves back and forth.

How We Hear Sound

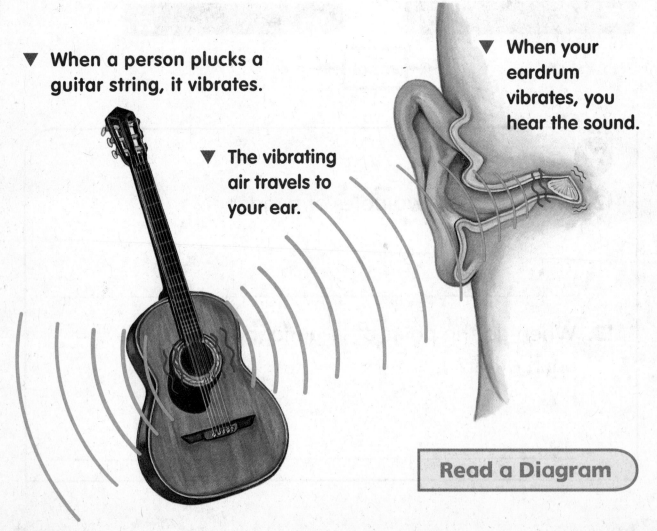

▼ When a person plucks a
guitar string, it vibrates.

▼ The vibrating
air travels to
your ear.

▼ When your
eardrum
vibrates, you
hear the sound.

Read a Diagram

When you speak, air moves from your lungs to your throat. The air moves over your vocal cords and causes them to vibrate. Touch your throat as you speak. What do you feel?

When you speak, your vocal cords vibrate.

◄ When you blow air through a flute, it vibrates and makes a sound.

✔ Quick Check

Fill in the blanks.

14. The part of your ear that vibrates is

the _____ .

15. When you speak, air moves from your lungs to

your _____ .

What makes sounds loud or soft?

When a sound is loud, the vibrations are big. When a sound is soft, the vibrations are small. When you yell, you make big vibrations in your throat. When you whisper, you make smaller vibrations.

A lion's roar is so loud that you can hear it up to 6 miles away.

A cat's meow is not as loud as a lion's roar.

Think about a lion's roar. When you are near a lion, its roar sounds loud. When you are far away, its roar sounds soft. The farther away you are from a sound, the softer is sounds.

✔ Quick Check

Complete the chart by naming 3 soft sounds and 3 loud sounds.

16.

Soft Sounds	Loud Sounds

What makes sounds high or low?

Sounds can be high, low, or in between. When a sound is low, the vibrations are slow. A cow's moo and a man's voice are examples of low sounds.

high sound

low sound

▲ When you hit a short bar, you make a high sound. When you hit a long bar, you make a low sound.

When a sound is high, the vibrations are fast. A cat's meow and a child's voice are examples of high sounds.

Which dog's bark is a higher sound? ▶

 Quick Check

Circle the answer.

17. Vibrations are fast when a sound is low.

true   false

18. When you hit a long bar, the vibrations are fast.

true   false

19. Vibrations are fast when a sound is high.

true   false

20. A child's voice makes a low sound.

true   false

Write the number of the correct definition
next to each word.

___ attract   ___ gravity   ___ machine   ___ repel

___ vibrates   ___ sound   ___ weight

___ ramp   ___ poles   ___ lever

1. a kind of energy you hear

2. pull objects made of iron

3. moves back and forth quickly

4. the amount of force an object has

5. It lets you use less force to lift something.

6. A simple _____ makes the force of your push
   or pull stronger.

7. the two parts of a magnet where its pull is the strongest

8. a force that pulls things toward each other

9. when two poles of magnets push away from each other

10. a machine that helps you move things to a higher place

Credits

Cover Photo: (bkgd, r) David Keith Jones/Images of Africa Photobank/Alamy; (inset) Joseph Van Os/Getty Images; (bkgd)Digital Vision/PunchStock.

Illustration Credits: All illustrations are by Macmillan/McGraw-Hill except as noted below:
68: (tl, tr) Emma Schachner.
69: (tl, tr) Emma Schachner.
98: (bc) Baily Lauerman

Photography Credits: All photographs are by Ken Cavanagh for Macmillan/McGraw-Hill or Dr. Parvinder Sethi for Macmillian/McGraw-Hill or Michael Scott for Macmillan/McGraw-Hill except as noted below:

1: (1) Peter Anderson/Dorling Kindersley; (3) The Anthony Blake Photo Library/Alamy; (4) Peter Gardner/Dorling Kindersley. 2: (bc) (flower)Derek Hall /Dorling Kindersley. 3: (cl) Dave G. Houser/Corbis; (cr) David Noton/Getty Images. 4: (bl) Andre Jenny/Alamy. 5: (tr) D. Hurst/Alamy; (cl) Ingram Publishing/Alamy. 6: (cr) PHOTOTAKE Inc./Alamy; (bl) Kim Taylor and Jane Burton/Dorling Kindersley. 7: (cl) DIOMEDIA/Alamy; (cr) PhotoAlto/PunchStock. 9: (tr) Malcolm Case-Green/Alamy. 10: (inset) Peter Gardner/Dorling Kindersley; (tr) Derek Hall/Dorling Kindersley; (inset) blickwinkel/Alamy; (bl) David Sieren/Visuals Unlimited. 11: (tr) Jane Grushow/Grant Heilman Photography. 12: (bl) Frans Lanting/Minden Pictures; (br) ©Darren Bennett/Animals Animals - Earth Scenes. 13: (tc) Andrew Beckett/Dorling Kindersley; (tr) Peter Haigh/Alamy. 14: (tr) Brand X Pictures/PunchStock; (cr) Papilio/Alamy; (bl) Gary Crabbe/Alamy; (br) Siede Preis/Getty Images. 15: (c) Russell Illig/Photodisc/Getty Images. 16: (cl) Doug Sokell/Visuals Unlimited; (inset) britishcolumbiaphotos.com/Alamy; (cr) Michael Orton/Getty Images; (inset) Tom Bean/Corbis; (bl) David R. Frazier Photolibrary, Inc./Alamy. 17: (tr) C.W. Biedel/Corbis; (cl) Peter Arnold Inc./Alamy. 18: (tr) Maryann Frazier/Photo Researchers, Inc.; (bc) Theo Allofs/zefa/Corbis. 20: (bl, br) John Kaprielian/Photo Researchers, Inc. 21: (tc) Fabrice Bettex/Alamy. 23: (2) Robert Maier/Animals Animals - Earth Scenes; (3) Wendell Metzen/Bruce Coleman; (4) John P. Marechal/Bruce Coleman; (5) John T. Fowler/Alamy; (6) Martin Harvey/Alamy. 24: (tr) Oswald Eckstein/zefa/Corbis; (cr) Dorling Kindersley; (bl) Angus Oborn/Rough Guides/Dorling Kindersley; (br) Frank Greenaway/Dorling Kindersley. 25: (c) Steve Hamblin/Alamy. 26: (bl) franzfoto.com/Alamy; (cr) Wendell Metzen/Bruce Coleman. 27: (tr) Danita Delimont/Alamy; (cl) Herve Berthoule/Jacana/Photo Researchers, Inc. 28: (tr) Bob Elsdale/Photonica/Getty Images; (cl) Dave King/Dorling Kindersley/Getty Images; (br) Jane Burton/Bruce Coleman. 29: (tr) Xavier Desmier/RAPHO/Imagestate. 30: (cl) Reuters/Corbis; (cr) Keren Su/China Span/Alamy; (bl) Michael L. Peck/Imagestate. 31: (tr) Natural Visions/Alamy. 32: (bc) Martin Harvey/Peter Arnold, Inc. 33: (cr) John Daniels/Ardea London Ltd. 34: (tr) Kim Taylor/Bruce Coleman; (tr) John B. Free/naturepl.com; (cl) Jeff Foott/naturepl.com; (br) Natural Visions/Alamy. 35: (tr) Joanna Van Gruisen/Ardea London Ltd. 38: (tl) Papilio/Alamy; (tr) John P. Marechal/Bruce Coleman. 39: (tl) John T. Fowler/Alamy; (tc) PHOTOTAKE Inc./Alamy; (tr) DIOMEDIA/Alamy. 40: (cl) AGEfotostock/SuperStock; (br) Ferrero-Labat/Ardea London Ltd. 41: (tc) Brand X Pictures/PunchStock. 42: (bc) Carson Baldwin Jr./Animals Animals - Earth Scenes. 43: (tl) Papilio/Alamy; (tr) Tom & Pat Leeson/Ardea London Ltd. 44: (bc) Martin Harvey/Alamy. 45: (tl) Peter Arnold, Inc./Alamy. 47: (1) Gary Will/Visuals Unlimited; (2) Colin Keates/Dorling Kindersley, Courtesy of the Natural History Museum, London; (3) Ken Lucas/Visuals Unlimited; (4) Mark A. Schneider/Photo Researchers, Inc.; (5) Lawrence Lawry/Photo Researchers, Inc.; (6) Gary Braasch/Corbis; (7) Per Karlsson - BKWine.com/Alamy. 48: (tl) Andreas Einsiedel/Dorling Kindersley; (tcl) Joyce Photographics/Photo Researchers, Inc.; (tcr) Mike Dunning/Dorling Kindersley; (tr)

Doug Martin/Photo Researchers, Inc.; (bl) Dorling Kindersley; (bcl) Colin Keates/Dorling Kindersley, Courtesy of the Natural History Museum, London; (bcr) Harry Taylor/Dorling Kindersley. 50: (tr) Harry Taylor/Dorling Kindersley; (bl,bc) Colin Keates/Dorling Kindersley, Courtesy of the Natural History Museum, London. 51: (tr) Colin Keates/Dorling Kindersley, Courtesy of the Natural History Museum, London; (cl) wsr/Alamy. 52: (cl) Mark A. Schneider/Photo Researchers, Inc.; (cr) Ken Lucas/Visuals Unlimited; (br) Harry Taylor/Dorling Kindersley. 53: (tr) Mike Dunning/Dorling Kindersley; (cr) Lawrence Lawry/Photo Researchers, Inc. 54: (bc) Gary Braasch/Corbis. 55: (tr) Tony Wheeler/Lonely Planet Images; (cl) David Keaton/Corbis. 56: (t to b) Boris Karpinski/Alamy. 57: (tl) bildagentur-online.com/th-foto/Alamy; (tr) Detlev van Ravenswaay/Photo Researchers, Inc. 58: (cr) Ingram Publishing/Alamy; (cr) Andrew Bargery/Alamy; (bl) Per Karlsson - BKWine.com/Alamy; (br) Holt Studios International Ltd/Alamy. 59: (tr) Craig Lovell - All Rights Reserved/Alamy. 60: (inset) Maurice Harmon/Graphistock/PictureQuest; (cl) Franck Jeannin/Alamy; (inset) Don Farrall/Getty Images; (bl) geogphotos/Alamy. 61: (cr) Mark & Audrey Gibson/Stock Connection; (inset) Matt Meadows/Peter Arnold, Inc. 62: (bc) Jane Burton/Dorling Kindersley. 63: (tr) McDonald Wildlife Photography/Animals Animals - Earth Scenes. 65: (1) Mark A. Schneider/Photo Researchers, Inc.; (2) ©The American Museum of Natural History; (3) D. Schwimmer/Bruce Coleman; (4) D. Schwimmer/Bruce Coleman. 66: (cr) Louie Psihoyos/Corbis; (bl) Mark A. Schneider/Photo Researchers, Inc. 67: (tr) Layne Kennedy/Corbis; (cl) Francois Gohier/Gaston Design/Photo Researchers, Inc. 70: (cr) James L. Amos/National Geographic Image Collection; (bl) Ken Lucas/Visuals Unlimited. 71: Peter Arnold, Inc./Alamy; (inset) Ken Lucas/Visuals Unlimited; (cl) Philip Lewis/Alamy. 72: (bc) Francis Latreille/Corbis. 73: (cr) Francis Latreille/Corbis. 74: (tr) Ted Soqui/Corbis SYGMA; (bc) Philip James Corwin/Corbis. 76: (cl) Francois Gohier/Photo Researchers, Inc.; (br) Kevin Schafer/NHPA. 77: (tc) B.A.E. Inc./Alamy. 79: (1) ML Sinibaldi/Corbis; (2) allOver photography/Alamy; (3) Lester Lefkowitz/Getty Images. 80: (bl) Mark A. Johnson/Corbis. 81: (tc) PhotoLink/Getty Images; (cl) Michael S. Yamashita/Corbis; (cr) Juliette Wade/Dorling Kindersley; (cr) Lester V. Bergman/Corbis. 82: (bc) Andy Sacks/Getty Images. 83: (tr) davies & starr/Getty Images; (cr) Demetrio Carrasco/Dorling Kindersley, Courtesy of the Hubbell Trading Post National Historic Site, Arizona; (bc) Timothy O'Keefe/Bruce Coleman. 84: (bc) Bettmann/Corbis; (inset) Lester Lefkowitz/Corbis. 85: (cr) ML Sinibaldi/Corbis. 86: (tr) Brand X Pictures/PunchStock; (tr) C Squared Studios/Getty Images; (bl) John Elk III/Lonely Planet Images/Getty Images; 86: (br) D. Hurst/Alamy. 87: (tl) Photodisc/PunchStock/Getty Images, Inc.; (tc) Gary Crabbe/Alamy; (tr) Becky Luigart-Stayner/Corbis. 88: (tr) Comstock Images/Alamy; (cr) Photodisc Collection/Getty Images; (cr) Ingram Publishing/Alamy; (bl) Royalty-Free/Corbis; (br) Bruton-Stroube Studios/FoodPix/PictureQuest. 89: (cr) allOver photography/Alamy. 90: (bc) Lester Lefkowitz/Getty Images. 91: (tr) Thinkstock/Alamy; Brand X Pictures/Alamy. 92: (bl) Craig Lovell/Corbis; (br) Mark Thomas/FoodPix/PictureQuest. 93: (tr) Royalty-Free/Corbis; (cl) Getty Images. 95: (3) Lester Lefkowitz/Corbis; (4) Mark Scott/Getty Images; (5) Rubberball/PictureQuest; (6) Norbert Schaefer/Corbis; (7) Rolf Bruderer/Corbis; (8) David Young-Wolff/Photo Edit. 99: (tl) Chris Mattison/Dorling Kindersley; (tr) Kim Taylor/Dorling Kindersley; (cr) Amos Morgan/Getty Images. 100: (tl, tr) Photodisc/Getty Images. 101: (tr) Photodisc/Getty Images. 102: (bc) Mark Scott/Getty Images. 103: (1) Photodisc/Getty Images; (2) Geoff Dann/Dorling Kindersley; (3) Digital Vision/PunchStock. 104: (bc) Rubberball/PictureQuest. 105: (tr) Norbert Schaefer/Corbis; (cl) Rolf Bruderer/Corbis. 106: (bc) Jeff Greenberg/Photo Edit. 108: (bc) David Young-Wolff/Photo Edit. 109: (tr) Royalty-Free/Corbis. 110: (cr) Robert W. Ginn/